Activity and Discussion Guide for

Abby Wize - Away

(Revised Edition)

Interfaith, Intergenerational, Flexible
Questions and Activities

By Lisa Bradley Godward

www.Wize.Media

©2021 Lisa Bradley Godward/ Wize Media
Reproduction for personal/fair use only

Please leave positive reviews on Amazon.com for this little book, and for the spiritual time-travel fantasy novel it goes with: *Abby Wize - AWAY*, even if you didn't obtain your book on Amazon.

www.amazon.com/dp/1733327606 for *Abby Wize - AWAY*, all three versions under that listing,
www.amazon.com/dp/1733327633 this Activity Guide in paper, and
www.amazon.com/dp/1733327640 in eBook format.

Reach out to author Lisa Bradley Godward on Facebook:
  Personal page: Abby Wize
  Fan Page for posting your Group news: Abby Wize Media

Website for book(s) and related products: www.wize.media . Email Ms. Godward through the website or directly at grow@wize.media .

Please spread the word about this positive, enlightened view of humanity's future! See section at end of this book. Contact Ms. Godward for video visits and more!

© Lisa Bradley Godward 2021

ISBN-13: 978-17333276-3-3 (paper)
ISBN-13: 978-17333276-4-0 (eBook)

First Printing Sept. 15, 2021

Printed By IngramSpark
Published by Wize Media

©2021 Lisa Bradley Godward/ Wize Media
Reproduction for personal/fair use only

Activity and Discussion Guide
Interfaith, Intergenerational, Flexible

Written by Lisa Bradley Godward

Symbols Guide:
💬 = Discuss
➪ = Activity to do
ⓘ = Research from books, people, the internet, etc., during your meetings, in advance, or afterward
📖 = Come back to this spot later/add to this item
⌨ = Type it up and post on Abby Wize Media's Facebook Fanpage
📷 = Photograph or scan and post this activity on the Abby Wize Facebook pages: "Abby Wize" and/or "Abby Wize Media." For video, post on YouTube and post the link to Abby's FB. Be sure not to use copyrighted music or images.
✉ = Email to Author Lisa Bradley at grow@wize.media .
⚲ = Notice a text tie-in on the book's cover
(p. X, ¢Z) = Discussion topic reference point in the novel (Kindle readers, use key search words and chapter headings)
Endnote = Refer to this Guide's numbered endnotes for additional information. Not to be confused with the Book's Endnotes.

—About the paragraph numbering system: any text at the top of a page counts as the first paragraph.—

<u>All activities are merely suggestions! Change as you wish!</u>

©2021 Lisa Bradley Godward/ Wize Media
Reproduction for personal/fair use only

Book Discussion and Activity Guide

Acknowledgements:

📖 Author Lisa Bradley Godward says *Harry Potter* author J.K. Rowling caused the seed of Abby Wize to sprout. (p. i, unmarked) After you read a few chapters, discuss: Do you see any *Harry Potter* influence on *Abby Wize*?

💬 Why do you think the author put endnotes in a work of fiction? Do you think you will like them or not?

Chapter 1: Moony

💬 What are your feelings about horses? (p. 1) Do you know much about horses? Do you know people who feel as Abby does about them?

💬 Is there something else besides horses that you are passionate about, like Abby is about horses? (pp. 1-2) Does your activity have a dangerous element, like horses do? How do you handle that?

💬 Are you sensitive to things, like Abby is to seams pressing into her? (p. 1, ¶3) What do you do to get things more to your liking?

💬 What do you do, or wish you did, when you're with people and something inappropriate comes along, like the lustful lyrics on the radio? (p. 2, ¶ 5)

💬 Are there times that you've been pretty sure people have been gossiping about you behind your back? (p. 1, ¶ 4 and p. 3, ¶ 6) How does that change your relationship with them after you suspect that? What do you think can be done to change this?

♀ Notice the horses on the cover and their tack (equipment).

➡ Use a soft rope, ribbon or belt to do the same steps Abby does in haltering a horse. One of you be the horse, and the other one Abby; then switch. (p. 4, ¶ 4)

➡ Act out Abby trying to get Moony walking, but only if you can be safe. It will be safer if the "horse" is much bigger than "Abby," like if the "horse" is an adult and "Abby" is a youth. (p. 4) Why do you think it finally works when she pulls hard from his side?

➡ ⓘ Use a long cord or rope to practice the quick-release knot on **http://www.thinklikeahorse.org/index-6.html** . (Scroll down to the third picture with the red lines). Enlarge the drawing to see the under or over directions. Because horses are unpredictable flight prey animals, it's safer to tie them in a way that can be undone quickly, in case the horse panics and then feels trapped.

Chapter 2: Riding

💬 Why does Tyler tell the kids to be the boss of the horse? (p. 7)

💬 Have you ever imitated something you saw in a photo or movie? (p. 7, last ¶) Did it go well or not?

⇨ Act out Abby's riding lesson, minus the fall. Keep it safe. (pp. 7-9)

💬 Have you ever had something bad yet good happen, like Abby winning the ribbon during her accident? (pp. 9-10)

💬 Have you ever been in a group where people are going out of their way to cover up or ignore something bad with rowdy jokes? (p. 10, ¶5) Does it work? Is there a better way?

Chapter 3: Home

⇨ Find a hallway with door trim and trail your fingers across open and/or closed doors as you walk, like Abby. (p. 11, last ¶)

💬 Have you ever been yelled at unfairly? (p. 12, ¶ 5-7) Adults: have you found yourself doing the yelling, and later regretted it? What strategies can we think of to avoid doing this when irritated and in positions of authority?

💬 Think of a time when you had to figure out an unclear command. (pp. 12-13) Were you ever eventually glad you had to figure it out? How/in what way?

⇨ Look deeply into your own eyes in a mirror (possibly when alone). (p. 13, ¶4) What do you see or feel?

💬 Have you ever been in a scouting program? (p. 16, ¶2) How do you feel about earning badges? What other groups (faith, school, or other) give accomplishment badges?

💬 Abby likes *Harry Potter*. Do you? (p. 17)

💬 Is it normal for siblings (brothers and sisters) to grow apart when they enter their teen years? Why or why not? (p. 18, ¶2)

💬 Do you have dreams like Abby's, in which you master beauty, control and power? (p. 18)

⇨ Draw one of your most powerfully positive dreams.

©2021 Lisa Bradley Godward/ Wize Media
Reproduction for personal/fair use only

Chapter 4: Church

💬 Why does Abby dress up for church? (p. 19) Do you dress up to go to special events? Why? What do you think is God's view of dressing up for religious events?

📍 The Wize's church is on the left edge of the back cover.

💬 ⓘ Does anyone you know have a favorite quilt? (p. 20, ¶ 2) Do you know anyone who quilts? Why might quilts, blankets and comforters be given to parents for their babies' births?

➡ Make a paper quilt (or fabric, if someone knows how) made of "blocks" of paper on which your Group draws pictures on a theme, such as "We are Peacemakers" or "Caring for the World and Each Other" or any other worthy theme. "Stitch" the "Blocks" together with colored duct or other wide tape, which will look like "sashing." Leave an inch of blank paper at the edge of the drawings to allow for the tape. Be sure each artist initials and dates their "block" in the lower right part. Display it at gatherings.

💬 What magazines do you like and why? (p. 20, ¶3)

💬 ⓘ What are your thoughts about animals being mistreated? (pp. 20, last two ¶) What religious writings discuss treatment of animals?

➡ ⓘ Print and illustrate some meaningful writings about animals. If possible, print the words with a calligraphy pen or brush.

➡ ⓘ "Mother ... wore a loose, lavender-colored linen skirt ...." (p. 21, ¶ 1) This sentence has alliteration, meaning several of the same sound, in this case, "L." Tongue-twisters use difficult alliteration. Share some tongue-twisters and identify the alliteration used. Example: Peter Piper picked a peck of pickled peppers. [Of course, to get your tang all tongueled up, you're s'posed to say it fast several times in a row!]

💬 ➡ Have you ever felt like someone treated you as a thing instead of a person? (p. 21, ¶4) Share the event if you wish. Have you ever realized you treated someone so that they felt like a thing instead of a person? What would be a better way to speak or act in situations like that? Roleplay both the less-respectful and the more-respectful interchanges.

➡ Write the Benediction (p. 24, last ¶) or another blessing you like in careful, attractive letters. Decorate it appropriately.

©2021 Lisa Bradley Godward/ Wize Media
Reproduction for personal/fair use only

💬 ⓘ Assistant Reverend Gottle did something shocking. (p. 26) Abby felt it didn't befit his position as a clergyman. How have other religions dealt with the fact that clergypeople are still human and might "sin"? Have you ever read any other books that deal with this theme, for example, *The Scarlet Letter* by Nathaniel Hawthorne?

💬 ⓘ Why does Mother deliver intimate news with the "tactfulness of a steamroller"? (p. 28 ¶ 12) Do you think you are (or will be) better, worse, or the same at talking about difficult, embarrassing or personal subjects with your children or parents? What kinds of intimate subjects might you need to be prepared to discuss with people at different stages of your life? [For example, as we enter puberty, it helps to know what physical and emotional changes we're going to experience. As we have babies of our own, we need quite a lot of information about pregnancy and birth and newborns. As we raise our own children, we will have to talk about many touchy subjects lovingly and openly. We may have to become caretakers for our own elderly parents, and may need to discuss death, funeral arrangements, living wills, and so on.] What sources of comfort, information and guidance do you think you will be able to turn to for discussing these delicate subjects?

💬 Mother insists that Abby pack her suitcase a certain way. (pp. 27-28) Have you ever had a different system for doing something than someone else? How do you deal with it when that person insists on having their way? How do you wish they (or you) would deal with it?

⇨ Role-play some situations after discussion from the previous question.

⇨ ⓘ Talk about what happens in our bodies when we have strong emotions, like Abby's lump in her throat on p. 29, second ¶ from the bottom. **https://www.sciencealert.com/why-do-we-get-a-lump-in-our-throats-when-we-re-sad** is one reference to research this universal human phenomenon.

⇨ 💬 Write a sentence or two detailing Abby's other possible physical reactions in this scene after learning more about them. Work together or separately, trying for the clearest, most meaningful descriptions. What skills do you notice are necessary to do this writing?

©2021 Lisa Bradley Godward/ Wize Media
Reproduction for personal/fair use only

💬 ⓘ Abby was forced to clean the bathroom at the scene of her humiliation. (p. 29, last ¶) Have you heard of people who have been required to pay for the bullets that killed a family member (Iran) or who had to pay money to police to recover the body of their loved one in order to mourn and bury them (China)? What human qualities are missing in these events?

Chapter 6: Driving

💬 ⇨ Abby and Jenn have a silent conversation using eye movements, tilts of their heads, and small expressions with their mouths. (p. 31, ¶1) This can happen when two people know each other very well. Have you ever been so in tune with someone that you can do this with them? Roleplay and film some. 📷

💬 Did you ever tell something to someone you trusted, but it was so hard to hear yourself say the whole truth, you held back something? Is this bad, good, or something else? Can truth sometimes be too hard to share all at once? Try to share some examples, either made-up (hypothetical) or real, if you feel comfortable doing so. [Whenever someone shares something personal of themselves, listeners must be respectful and never repeat it to someone outside of the Group. Group members should also be careful with extremely sensitive information until it is known that others can be trusted – often an undeveloped skill.]

⇨ Try a Sodoku puzzle as a group. (p. 33, ¶7) Who hasn't ever done one before? Who has? Do you like it or not? Why? [It's important to know what we like and don't like, have or don't have a natural talent for.]

💬 Are there foods you don't like? (pp. 34-35) Why do you suppose people like or don't like foods?

⇨ Find out what foods pretty much everybody likes and see about having them at one of your meetings. See what's the healthiest food you can manage. See about making some food together.

💬 Mother apparently feels that outward appearances are more important than inward qualities. (p. 35, last ¶) What do you think?

⇨ ⓘ Try drawing some Appaloosa horses like Abby does. (p. 36, ¶3) There are different kinds of Appaloosa spots, each with their own names. Learn about them on http://www.appaloosamuseum.org/spotting-patterns-in-appaloosas/ or other horse breed reference works.

Chapter 7: Sofia

💬 ⓘ Aunt Sofia (so-FYE-uh) says, "Many hands make light work." (p. 37, ¶4) What sayings, principles or ideas guide you and/or your family?

💬 It's been said that "Hurt people hurt people." In what ways might Mother have been hurt that she acts like this? (p. 38, ¶ 3)

⇨ ⓘ Help everyone in your group see a game of *Magic: The Gathering*, whether live or recorded. (p. 39, ¶ 6) Why has it remained popular since its invention in 1993? Author Lisa Bradley Godward hopes to create a similar game; email her ✉ if you're interested in helping.

💬 Are Carol, Barb and Penny gossiping? (p. 39) What is gossip? Is it mean to gossip about TV or computer personalities like that?

💬 Do you feel behind the times when someone has a newer gadget than you? (p. 40, ¶5) Are you satisfied with your usual – or latest – response in these situations? If not, what's a better response?

💬 Abby admires many of Hakene Bodant's (a fictitious name) inner qualities. (pp. 40-43) Do you think she admires his confidence because she lacks that quality? If so, do you think people often admire qualities they don't have? If not, why does she admire his abilities?

💬 Abby bails out of a social situation that proves too much for her. (p. 41, ¶6) If you were in Abby's situation or a similar one, what would you do and why?

⇨ Role play the situation from the previous question. 🎦

💬 What do you think of the agreement that Penny and her younger brother, Ricky, make? (p. 42) Why do you think that? Would it have been better for one or both of them to handle it another way? If so, what way?

💬 ⓘ Abby and Jenn usually think that when movies are made from books, the books are better than the movies. (p. 43, ¶3) What do you think? Name examples. **www.imdb.com** is a useful site for researching movies and the books they're based on.

⇨ Watch a movie and read the book it came from. Be prepared to explain which one was better or worse and why you think so. ⌨

⇨ ⓘ Look up the word *femmes*. (p. 45, ¶5) What does it mean, in what language, and have you seen it before? Why might the author have used it instead of similar words? ⌨

💬 What do you think of Jenn's explanation of nakedness? (pp. 43-44) If God created us noble and beautiful and in His image, why do we wear clothes and feel embarrassed about our nakedness?

⇨ ⓘ Find and share some different philosophies and viewpoints on the human form. Possible sources might be religions, sculptors, and doctors/medical sources.

💬 Jenn helps Abby understand some of Abby's tangled feelings. (pp. 43-45) A great book or movie helps explain us to ourselves in an interesting, nonthreatening way. What books, movies, etc., have helped you figure out more about yourself, your family, the purpose of life, etc.?

⇨ ⓘ Puberty can be a difficult time with bodily changes in boys and girls. (pp. 44-45) It helps a lot to have someone you can turn to with questions that books, health classes, or parents don't answer. Can you think of someone you can turn to? If any of you are willing to be a source of information for each other, say so. If any of you wouldn't mind having someone to take your questions to, speak up. If the Group would like to have a question-and-answer session about puberty, fertility, sex, marriage, and related questions on reproduction, plan it. It can be done mostly anonymously, with questions submitted on slips of paper. There may be knowledgeable people willing to come and answer your questions. Childbirth educators, doctors, midwives, mothers, fathers, health care workers, school teachers, and more might be knowledgeable and willing to help, possibly by video call. Or if your Group is dealing with other physical or medical issues, discuss, find and share information on those topics.

⇨ How do you see God, fate, your future? (p. 45, last ¶) Is your faith a loving or a punitive one? Pair up and ask each other about these or other beliefs. See if you can boil your answer(s) down to two sentences or less. Ask if you find you need help.

Chapter 8: Vacation

💬 Jon isn't making much sense talking to Abby at breakfast. (pp. 47-49) But he seems to be very happy with the conversation, even making some important discoveries and connections for himself. Why did this happen? What did Abby do or not do? Have you ever had something similar happen? Could you employ some strategies to encourage deep sharing in the future?

💬 What was Ricky beginning to say? (p. 50, ¶2) Why did he change his wording? Have you ever done that? What would be some good and some bad reasons to change your wording like that?

💬 Did you ever wonder what it would be like to have been born into another family? (p. 51, ¶3)

➡ ⓘ Pick a culture, race, place or other characteristic that interests you. Imagine, or research, what it would be like to grow up or live there.

Chapter 9: Horseplay

♀ Notice Angie and Beauty on the back cover.

➡ Next time you clip your fingernails, set a clipping aside and watch it slowly dry out and curl. Horses' hooves do the same thing. (p. 53, ¶ 3) We wouldn't think there's any moisture in a hard nail or hard hoof, but there is. [Has anyone been to the Bahá'í World Center and seen Bahá'u'lláh's nail clippings?]

💬 Have you ever met anyone who seemed to cut another person down when it was actually a cover for expressing admiration? (p. 55, ¶ 2) How did you react to them? Share some other ways to respond to this.

💬 ⓘ ➡ Abby realizes she's done something wrong and her heart sinks. (pp. 56, ¶1) Since we're human and can never know everything, how should we handle it when we realize we've made a mistake? What about when the mistake affects another person? an animal? Research the proper steps of a true apology, such as at **https://www.huffpost.com/entry/4-steps-to-a-sincere-apology_b_6646346** .

Role play some situations that allow you to apologize using the steps of apology.

⇨ Act out Angie's play session with Beauty. (pp. 53-60) Pair up; one of you be the horse, the other the trainer. Compare with the attitude and feeling you had/think you would have during the horseplay exercise in Chapter 1. You might enjoy referring to the pretty flower-like map of emotions at
https://simple.wikipedia.org/wiki/List_of_emotions , and to **https://www.virtuesproject.com/virtueslist.html** for personal traits.

💬 Angie says a good horse whisperer should know how to be firm, fair, and friendly in turns, as needed. (p. 60, third ¶ from bottom) Do you think this could apply to handling people, too? Why or why not? If you got good with horses (or other animals), would it help you handle people well? Why or why not?

Chapter 10: Bookstore

💬 Have you ever seen a jalopy like Jon's? (pp. 62-63) What might it say about the owners? What doesn't it say?

⇨ Directions to make the design Melissa stitches on p. 63 are given on pp. 294-305. Try one or both of the counted cross-stitch designs in the back of the book.

⇨ 📖..Why might Abby have thought the painting of 'Abdu'l-Bahá looked like Dumbledore? (p. 64, ¶4) Compare portraits of both, perhaps by Googling. Discuss Abby's growing understanding of each of these men (one real, one fictitious) as she learns more.

💬 If you knew nothing about 'Abdu'l-Bahá, would you be able to tell that he was from the Middle East just by looking at a picture of him? (p. 64) Why or why not?

⇨ Find and compare pictures and/or drawings of different styles of dress from around the world. Which ones look comfortable? Uncomfortable? Practical? Ceremonial? Find out how that costume developed, and any symbolism or significance to its various features.

⇨ Visit one, or have your own, art show (p. 65) of spiritually-inspired art in many mediums (materials). Make a sign next to each work telling about it.

⇨ Using a real, substitute or imaginary fountain, make good wishes and toss a real or imagined coin in. (pp. 65-66) How many ways can you toss? [A substitute fountain could be a kiddie wading pool, a real pool, or even a bowl of water. An imaginary fountain … well, it's however everyone imagines it to be, which could be a fun exercise in itself!]

⇨ If it's okay with everyone and you stay under control, recreate the "crossing" scene on pp. 65-66.

🛈 Notice Melissa and Jon at the fountain in the middle of the back cover, and on the interior illustration on page 70.

⇨ Act out the mood changes on page 66. [One of the most rewarding things about a good book is the emotional journey we go on; this is one of the dips in the road. By having downer moments, we appreciate the higher spots.]

💬 What do you think of the Native American quote on p. 67? Is there an animal, tree, plant or spot that speaks to your heart?

💬 ⓘ What other names are there for God, such as Wakantanka? (p. 67) Find some and discuss the information surrounding each. [One source: **http://en.wikipedia.org/wiki/Names_of_God**]

💬 Abby's family doesn't have much extra money, and she's intimidated by the riches she sees in one upscale magazine. (p. 68, ¶3) Have you ever felt that way? Is there another way to look at this, so you don't feel intimidated and "less than"?

💬 Have you ever wanted something for a noble purpose, and it came to you unexpectedly? (p. 69, ¶5) Discuss wanting something for a noble purpose versus other kinds of wanting. What is materialism? How can we combat it?

Chapter 11: News

💬 What Titanic song is Abby singing on p. 71? There are two famous Titanic Songs; one is from the 1997 movie, sung by Celine Dion; the other is a much older song popular at camps. Why do we sometimes make jokes and irreverent songs out of tragedies?

⇨ Find and sing both versions. For the movie version, try **http://www.youtube.com/watch?v=9J3bSdiHTP0** and **http://www.youtube.com/watch?v=RQKZQ3u7cdo** for the camp version (there are lots of variations on this song, as often happens with folk tunes).

💬 What do you think about the description of Oglala Sioux conversation methods from Luther Standing Bear? (p. 72) Have you ever met anyone who seems to speak this way?

⇨ Try Luther Standing Bear's speaking style (p. 72) for half an hour with your Discussion Group. Evaluate it afterwards. If you all like it, use it more! If you don't like it, say why.

💬 Abby is learning how to use a computer better on pp. 72-73. Have you ever figured out a piece of equipment on your own? What strategies or techniques did you use to figure it out? For example, you read the manual, you Googled it, you studied the equipment, you tried a few things to see which worked, etc.

⇨ Abby makes a "babyish rhyme" of her very own on p. 73, ¶4 – "Fly from sad and bad, ride to glad!" Make some of your own meaningful mottos and sayings. Write them someplace special in a special way, such as on a card in colorful pens, or in a journal using abbreviations, codes, or pictograms. 📷

Chapter 12: Flying

💬 Abby had had a vague feeling she wanted to bring her boots and jeans, but couldn't justify it to Mother. (p. 27, last ¶) On p. 76, ¶4, she finds out why she'd have been better off bringing them. Have you ever had a feeling you should do something, and later found out why it was a good idea? Why does this happen? How can we know if we should listen to those ideas or not?

💬 The italicized sentence at the bottom of p. 77 is Abby's prayer as she's in the middle of an accident. Describe the panicked prayers you've uttered or thought.

⇨ Act out Abby's horseback ride in Chapter 12, being careful not to hurt anyone or anything.

Chapter 13: Friend

💬 Dali and Abby have a hard time understanding each other at first. Why? What causes it to eventually get better? Have you ever had this kind of conversation with someone? Did it get better? Why?

💬 📖 After you read the book, come back to Dali's nonsensical statement on p 80, ¶2. What do you think she was trying to say?

©2021 Lisa Bradley Godward/ Wize Media
Reproduction for personal/fair use only

💬 What impression do you get about Dali from her house? Are houses a reflection of their occupants? Why or why not?

ⓘ ⇨ Look at some TRAIL OF PAINTED PONIES figurines (p. 81, second ¶ from bottom) at **www.TrailofPaintedPonies.com** . Which ones do you like? Draw one you'd like to make. Or buy a kit to actually paint one: Google "paint your own horse kit."

⇨ ⓘ Sound out the sound box's sounds. (p. 81, second ¶ from bottom) Put a steady beat to it; try fast and slow, loud and soft. Invent your own sound sequences that Abby might have heard. Listen to some New Age soundscapes to give you some ideas. Go to iTunes store, iHeartRadio, TuneIn or similar services and search New Age, Soundscapes, Steve Roach, Moon Milne, Adam Lastiwka or other artists making the kind of sounds Abby might have heard.

💬 Why do you think Dali says "the area of North Carolina" instead of just "North Carolina"? (p. 82, 6th ¶ from bottom)

⇨ 📖 Make a list, talk about, act out, or draw a picture of your vision of an ideal world. (p. 83, ¶6 and 7) Not someone else's that you've seen in a movie, but your own thoughts. Save it and look at it again after you've read this book. Did any of your ideas change? Redraw, revise, or rediscuss your concept if so.

💬 By the end of this chapter (p. 86), what do you know about the *Abby Wize* world of the future? Would you like to go there? Why or why not?

Chapter 14: Town

💬 Have you ever used a different kind of toilet from the usual American ones? (p. 87)

⇨ ⓘ Research and report on why sanitation is a very important topic. What is the name of the career that designs and builds sewage systems? What happens when sewage gets into food and water?

💬 What do you think of UL? (p. 88, first few ¶) Do you wish we had that now? Why or why not?

⇨ ⓘ Use the online dictionary at **www.lernu.net** or Google Translate, which Lisa Bradley Godward used to come up with words for this book. Plug in different words in English. Make sure the translation says "English –Eo" (English to Esperanto). Investigate Esperanto further. Learn a few phrases.

ⓘ 💬 Look at some English from 700 years ago. (p. 88 ¶4) Can you read it? Discuss.

💬 Have you ever ridden double on a single bicycle? (p. 89, bottom)

⇨ ⓘ Find a picture of, or actually try out, a double-bicycle. Listen to the classic song, *A Bicycle Built for Two* by searching for it in music sources such as **www.YouTube.com** .

💬 ⇨ Discuss Dali's divine prompting she wishes she'd listened to. (p. 89, last ¶) Try to imagine the scene in which she had that prompting and ignored it. Try writing that scene. ⌨

⇨ Pretend you enter one or more of the auxiliaries. (p. 92, ¶ 8-12) What would they be like? Roleplay this and/or write a new scene about it. Readers/fans writing additional scenes is called "Fan Fiction." Try more scenes than just the ones suggested here! ⌨ 📷

⇨ Make, or help make, a mural like on p. 92, 6ᵗʰ ¶ from the bottom. Yours could be permanently painted on a surface (wall, bridge, etc.) or temporarily mounted, such as paper or fabric pieces taped or sewn together and hung for a shorter display. Decide on a theme and a style. Plan how it will be done first. ⌨ 📷

💬 If there's no crime and no need for security measures in Erden (*AIR-den*), why does Dali press her finger to an electronic pad? (p. 93, 6ᵗʰ ¶ from bottom)

ⓘ 💬 Look up the words Anagogic, Esthesis, and Recourse, from which the author made the AerY name. (p. 94, ¶5) Why might she have chosen those? Is this finally the high-tech stuff Abby had been expecting? Discuss. ⌨

💬 What other synonyms for "cool" can you think of besides those listed on p. 94, 10ᵗʰ ¶ from the bottom? Do they have other common meanings? How do words change and get used as slang?

💬 Why do you think the Bahá'í Writings (and other Writings) say that disadvantaged people are special and should be protected? (p. 94, third ¶ from bottom) ⌨

Chapter 15: Library

⇨ 📖 After you read the book, come back to the ALLY program listings (p. 96, ¶2) and add your own invented channels. ⌨

⇨ Play Solitaire with actual cards; show those who don't know how. (p. 96, ¶3)

💬 What do you think of the "Consultation Today" show? (pp. 96-99) Can you think of any advantages to becoming skilled in spiritual consultation like this?

⇨ Act out the consultation scene.

⇨ Learn the Bahá'í steps to successful consultation and practice them with your Discussion Group. **Reference this Guide's Endnote 1.** The Group moderator can act as Chairperson. You can elect officers and pretend you're a Bahá'í Local Spiritual Assembly if you have at least 5 members in your Discussion Group.

Chapter 16: Pollution

⇨ Read carefully the description of Lodlan's House of Worship, (p. 101, ¶8-10) then draw it. 📷

❡ The House of Worship on the cover and on p. 108 is one artist's conception from this description. Yours can be different.

⇨ ⓘ Search for examples of half-timbered houses. (p. 101, ¶8) Feel free to use these images to assist your drawings of the House of Worship.

💬 ⇨ Pretend Abby went into the House of Worship. (pp. 101-102) What might it have been like? Draw or describe. ⌨ 📷

💬 Pretend Abby had been a religion other than Christian. (Bottom half of p. 102) What do you think Dali would have said? ⌨

💬 ⓘ Discuss using a universal pronoun such as "Sia" for God. (p. 102-103) Do other faiths or languages already do this, or something like it?

💬 Are there prayers, pledges or other sayings you've said without thinking about? (p. 103, ¶6) If so, go through them slowly and try to understand.

💬 What do you think about Dali's discussion on pollution causing mental as well as physical dysfunction? (p. 104, ¶2) Look up Book Endnotes 40 and 41. What might be done about these difficulties?

💬 Discuss other examples of science and religion agreeing. (pp. 106-107)

Chapter 17: Dream
💬 ➪ Discuss and/or act out the dream on pp. 109.. [Author Lisa Bradley Godward actually dreamed this!] What do you think it could mean to Abby? To Erden?

💬 ➪ ⓘ Discuss and/or draw other powerfully positive dreams you've had. Research, discuss and/or draw important dreams in the history of religion and human progress.

💬 Name the emotions and/or virtues we see in Abby during this short but very important chapter.

Chapter 18: Service
➪ Invent a tune for the prayer Dali sings on p. 113. Give it a good beat, one that would go nicely with the rhythm of bicycling. Accompany your song with drums and/or instruments. 📷

💬 ⓘ Research and/or talk about different religions' prayer requirements, such as the Bahá'í Obligatory Prayers or the Muslim requirement to pray five times a day. (p.113) Which ones have you said? Why do you think God would direct His children to pray?

➪ Try practicing 10 minutes of your Group session in the calm, thoughtful way portrayed in the second-to-last paragraph on p. 113. Everyone would keep their speaking short (less than two minutes), and should gather their thoughts first. Afterward, discuss how it felt to speak (and listen) this way. See about continuing to practice this in future Discussion Groups (or at home, maybe with pets!). 📷

💬 ⓘ Do you have to sit cross-legged with candles in a quiet, dark room to meditate properly? (p. 115, second from last ¶) What are some ways to meditate? What faiths or belief systems have helpful information on meditating?

➪ Practice different ways of meditating during a Group meeting. Yoga instructors, spiritual leaders, and others could help you with something short, whether in person, by video tutorial you share with the group, or by video calling during a meeting.

💬 Discuss whether kids might still trample flowers and be hard on grass in 700 years in a supposedly perfect world. (p. 116, ¶5)

⇨ Make up some dirt-digging songs the volunteers might have known and sung. (p. 116-117) 🎙️ ⌨️

⇨ ⓘ Listen to a real mandolin if you can; if not, look up some mandolin-family music on Youtube and/or read about lute-family developments on websites such as **https://en.wikipedia.org/wiki/History_of_lute-family_instruments** (p. 117, ¶1)

💬 Did the workers really mean a mudfight, were they joking, or was there a mistranslation? (p. 117, ¶4)

💬 Abby finds herself feeling great fondness for Mr. Sawqui. (p. 117, second-to-bottom ¶) Discuss any "oldens" you feel the same way about. Why do you feel that way?

⇨ Silently or out loud, decide on a way to tell a special "olden" how you feel about them. Be sure to make it realistic; plan something you can actually do. Simple is good, as long as it happens. If the Group wishes, set aside time during the Group meeting to plan and/or create this gesture, as a group or individually: a special memento, a letter, a poem, take (or copy or interpret) a meaningful picture, or other project.

⇨ 💬 Say the Medium Obligatory Prayer, perhaps first watching someone do it for teaching purposes. (p. 118, first several paragraphs) Discuss afterwards.

💬 ⇨ Discuss pilgrimages made in different faiths. (p. 120, ¶7) Describe any you've been on, whether official or not. If the Group wishes, bring a few pictures to share. Keep it brief or schedule another meeting to discuss pilgrimages in depth.

💬 ⓘ Abby realizes that the word "Indian" can mean a Native American or someone from India. (p. 120, ¶9) Do you know why the same word refers to people across the world from each other? If not, find out why and discuss this and other instances of how the world has been changed and affected for centuries because of the actions of a few people.

💬 ⇨ Name other homophones. (p. 121, ¶2) Make up and act out your own scenes in which confusions arise due to hearing, not reading, two homophones. ⌨️ 🎙️

©2021 Lisa Bradley Godward/ Wize Media
Reproduction for personal/fair use only

Chapter 19: Creation

💬 Discuss one thing that would cause children to feel less like third-class citizens in different countries. (p. 123, third from last ¶) Adults, did you feel that way as a child? How can you prevent doing the same thing to another child, since by seeing it or experiencing it, you may have been imprinted with that behavior? Discuss a reasonable middle ground between denying children a safe and healthy upbringing on the one hand and overindulging on the other hand.

➪ Draw your version of the "Auntie Zoray" banner. (p. 124, fourth paragraph from the bottom) Animate it with computer graphics if you're really advanced! 📷

➪ Write your own letter to Auntie Zoray, pretending you're someone from Erden. (pp. 124-126) Answer it if you want an even better challenge! ⌨

➪ Make your own creation out of the same or similar materials Abby uses. (pp. 126-127) You'll need to use glue or another Earther technique to secure the materials.

💬 Discuss the difference between little white lies, and the steering that Dali describes (p. 129, last ¶) Are they necessary? Are they good, bad, or something else? Should we develop these modes of speech or not?

💬 What would your calling name be? (p. 129, middle paragraphs) Discuss if you wish.

💬 ➪ 📖 Abby gains skills and grows her virtues by the end of this chapter. Describe some. Keep a list and add to it as you read of more ways in which she becomes more awake and aware.

Chapter 20: Party

➪ Draw the animated wallpaper border from page 131, ¶3 & 4. Add your own details. 📷

➪ Draw the people Abby might see on page 131, ¶6. 📷

💬 What are some of the odder names you've encountered? (p. 132, first four paragraphs) How do people feel when their names are made fun of?

➪ Draw a portrait of Kreshi from the descriptions on pages 132-133 (and other pages). 📷

ⓘ ⇨ Find pictures of people who decorate themselves in ways that are unusual to you. Try some of the safe, removable, temporary decorations.

💬 Why does Dali say that tacos and fried rice are mix-and-match? (p. 133, 3rd ¶ from bottom) Name more foods from other countries.

⇨ ⓘ Have an International Food meal and identify the origin of the dishes. (Could do this by meeting at a food court.) Determine the country the ingredients might have come from; for example, where the spices may have originally come from. Each of you could discuss one dish or one component of a dish as it relates to a particular country or region of a country. [Someone order tacos and enjoy the messiness of an un-twrapped taco!] (pp. 133-135)

⇨ Draw the Kingdom Coins on p. 134, ¶4-6. Or invent your own and draw those! 📷

💬 Monarch-of-the-mountain is the gender-neutral version of King of the Hill. (p. 135, ¶3) Name other games that used to be male-dominated (or still are) and needn't be. ⌨

ⓘ ⇨ Research kelpies. (p. 135, ¶4) Draw some. 📷

💬 Recycling, reducing and reusing are standard practices in Erden. (p. 135, second ¶ from bottom, etc.) Have you seen any stores that are set up for this now? The author noticed separately labeled containers for compost (food); washable dishes and utensils; paper recyclables; and trash at a Panera Bread store in Issaquah, Washington while on book tour in the summer of 2011, so some eateries are doing this now. Have you seen any? What do you do for the planet? What more could you do, realistically?

⇨ The group activity in the large back room seems like a combination of dance and martial arts. (pp. 135-136) Design and act out this exercise. Discuss and/or perform the prior and proper preparation those dancers would probably need to do in order to execute that exercise. ⌨ 📷

💬 While writing the passage on p. 136, ¶ 5, Author Lisa Bradley Godward looked up state laws to see when smoking bans were enacted and was surprised to find that even in 2007 (when the book takes place), smoking was permitted in a large number of places. What do you think can (or will) be done to limit or eliminate smoking in the decades to come?

©2021 Lisa Bradley Godward/ Wize Media
Reproduction for personal/fair use only

ⓘ ⇨ Do, or watch someone do, a DDR in person or on YouTube. (p. 136, second ¶ from bottom) Then pair up: one of you play the part of the silhouette dancer (dressed in black?) while the other tries to imitate the silhouette. Warm up slowly first, and allow for a slow cooling-down period after strenuous activity. Is there a scoring system with the Erdean game? Do you think there should be? Why or why not? If not, should there be something else to help the player feel a sense of accomplishment? If not, why? If so, what?

Chapter 21: Dragons
 ⓘ Several different hand motions have been described: saluting, (p. 138, second-to-last ¶) greeting, (p. 139, ¶3) and more. What are some other gestures of greeting from around the world?
⇨ Draw a portrait of Rykier. (pp. 139 on)
⇨ Have you ever had a fabulous time with friends like Abby does in this chapter? Describe. Draw or write about it, or act it out.

⇨ Act out the Riding Game (pp. 140-143).
⇨ Draw or film any part of the Riding Game (pp. 142-145).
Have you ever been teased in an unkind way? Is the banter and light teasing between Abby, Rykier and Kreshi acceptable or not? (p. 140 on) What makes it acceptable or not?
⇨ Rewrite one or more scenes as if Rykier and/or Kreshi were mean and their teasing was not fun; now rewrite them as if they didn't tease or joke at all. Discuss afterward: how does the tone change? What do you like or not like about the new scenes?
The author imagined that when people are careful not to hurt each other with unkind words, people will feel more free to express themselves comfortably; therefore she wrote "the guys sat watching (Abby) with small, silly smiles fixed on their unself-conscious faces." (p. 144, ¶ 10) Do you agree? What other changes would happen in societies if people weren't afraid of criticism or ridicule?
Discuss a typical American Christmas. (pp. 144, ¶11) How does materialism play into this major Christian holiday? How could it be brought back into the realms of reasonable?

©2021 Lisa Bradley Godward/ Wize Media
Reproduction for personal/fair use only

💬 Do you think that Erdeans would be able to sense what others are thinking or feeling, more than in the early 21ˢᵗ Century? If not, what would the interpersonal interactions be like? If so, would it be spirit-powered, yuter-powered, or something else? (pp. 144-147)

💬 Kreshi describes how Erdeans blend technological help with divine assistance. (p. 145, ¶ 8-13) How have you, or might you, do something similar?

💬 Compare Abby's sudden realization of Dali's difficult guiding (p. 145, third-from-last ¶) with the original event on pp. 79-84. Now that you've "been" in Erden a while, has your awareness become less like Abby's and more like Dali's? If so, how?

💬 Discuss at least one way Erdeans have solved crime. (p. 147, bottom third)

➪ 📖 Make a list of things Erdeans do to extend their lives and keep healthy. (p. 148, third ¶ from bottom) Add to it as you find more clues.

➪ What other words do different faiths use to try to get at this intangible idea of getting Divine Guidance? (midway down p. 149 through p. 151) Start your own personal list of wording that you find that seems to describe this spiritual plugging in.

Chapter 22: Happiness

💬 What is a twelve-step program that Kreshi refers to? (p. 153, ¶8) Why does he say it as if he was at an Earther funeral?

💬 Discuss "positive addictions." (p. 147, fifth paragraph from the bottom, and p. 153, ¶4 and 10, etc.)

💬 ➪ Have you had any Scripture-based, or spiritually influenced, fantasies or dreams? (p. 154, ¶3) Share, draw, etc. ⌨️ 🎙️

➪ Make and share your own chocolate (or any other) sampler plates. (p. 154, ¶4)

💬 Rykier says that everybody loves where they are on vacation; he implies that it's different when you live there. (p. 154, 3ʳᵈ and 5ᵗʰ ¶ from the bottom) Do you agree or disagree? Have you ever experienced this yourself? Discuss.

💬 Rykier says that in Erden, they can repair or replace almost every body part that could be damaged. (p. 155, ¶1) How might they do this?

💬 Abby definitely had the impression that when Peace arrived on Earth, there would be an end to suffering. (p. 24, 4ᵗʰ ¶ from bottom) Yet the Bahá'í Writings seem clear on the ongoing reality of tests, suffering and problems in this world. (p. 155, ¶ 5) How can these two seemingly opposing views be reconciled? **Refer to Guide Endnote 2.**

💬 Virtues material (p. 155) was taken from "The Virtues Project," created in 1991 by Linda Kavelin Popov, Dr. Dan Popov and John Kavelin, **www.VirtuesProject.com** . Do you have some virtues you think you're doing pretty well at? Which ones do you think you could use more of? Make a plan to improve at least one virtue. Page 155, ¶6 implies that everyone can use more patience. Discuss how to grow more patience and other attributes.

💬 What is the original saying that Abby modifies? (p. 156, ¶5) Do you have some favorite sayings? Any from spiritual origins, or are they secular (non-religious) in origin?

💬 Abby keeps realizing how living to 150 years old changes life in Erden compared to Earth. (p. 156, last ¶ and others) Can you think of other effects besides what she notices?

💬 A group arrives at the Draggin' Dragon to celebrate one boy's Accomplishment. (p. 157, fourth ¶ from bottom) In the Original Edition, the author had him celebrating a birthday. (p. 159, ¶ 6) Not all cultures and faiths celebrate birthdays. (**http://en.wikipedia.org/wiki/Birthday** , see Islam and Christianity/Jehovah's Witness) Why not? What do you think?

⇨ Draw an almacorn. (p. 158, top half) That's a mistake the author fixed in the Revised Edition: combining all three creatures would result in an almacorn, not an alacorn, as written in the Original Edition. (p. 159, ¶8) 🎨

💬 What else might Abby have seen in the wallpaper if she'd looked longer? (p. 158, top half) ⌨

💬 To the more mature readers in the Group: could a love relationship work out between Abby and Kreshi, assuming she stayed in Erden? (p. 158, last ¶) Name some problems and whether you think they would be surmountable or not.

⇨ Draw the Lodlan House of Worship as it looks at night. (p. 159, ¶6) 📷

💬 Do you think people should wait until they're married to have sex? (p. 159, bottom half) Some people claim it is not realistic to expect people to wait. What do you think? Have you heard of the "True Love Waits" campaign? Discuss.
http://www.lifeway.com/True-Love-Waits/c/N-1z13wiu

⇨ Look up a list of books that tells HOW to wait while dealing with sexual urges, such as the Christian books *Every Young Woman's Battle* and *Every Young Man's Battle* by Shannon Ethridge & Stephen Arterburn.

💬 What do you think about Erdeans marrying at age 15? (p. 159, second ¶ from bottom)

💬 Discuss Dali's confession that Erdeans are still human and still make mistakes. (p. 161, ¶ 2)

💬 Imagine how Dali might advise Abby about dating Kreshi. (p. 161, bottom half)

💬 Have fun assigning different foods to some religions and philosophies. (p. 162, second to last ¶)

Chapter 23: Deepening

⇨ Try eating food that's like Erdean food. (p. 165, ¶9, and others)

💬 How does Dali's way of handling intimate and sensitive issues differ from Mother's? (p. 166, ¶1 and p. 28, ¶6)

⇨ Act out Mother's part in a more loving, kind, and sensitive way.

💬 The author and original editor thought advanced technology might relieve pressure in fault lines to prevent major earthquakes; divert comets, asteroids, and meteors from outer space; and disperse hurricanes, tornadoes and typhoons. (p. 166, third ¶ from bottom and p.167, ¶9) Can you think of more problems that appropriate technology could solve? ⌨

💬 Have you ever noticed that when you're doing some mindless chore, helpful thoughts come to you? (p. 167, ¶ 3) Why do you think this happens?

⇨ Practice the door-closing command, and pretend it works to close a door. (p. 167, second ¶ from bottom) Tie on a string or fishing line, or have someone push it shut. What other capabilities do you think Erdeans would create in their homes, and which ones wouldn't they, given Dali's explanations about selective technology?

💬 How many of the analytical methods listed on pp. 168, top half, exist now? Have you or anyone you know used any of them? Why does Abby think they're "fruity?" What did you think? Read Arthur Schopenhauer's opinion of the cycle that new ideas often go through: "All truth passes through three stages: First, it is ridiculed; Second, it is violently opposed; and Third, it is accepted as self-evident." Discuss with examples and opinions.

💬 Discuss the Erdean idea of preventing crime through universal education and counseling of wrong-doers. (p. 169, ¶ 6 and p. 170, two-thirds down the page) Why not pass laws to rid the world of bad things and bad people?

💬 Discuss the idea of the Twin Processes. (p. 171, ¶ 6) Can you see evidence of both processes around you?

⇨ Role play an additional scene wherein Abby asks Dali, "How did the people from my hometime keep on, as things got worse? It seems so hopeless!" (p. 171, bottom ¶)

⇨ Call your Discussion Group together with a small gong and a small wooden mallet. (p. 172, 1st ¶)

💬 Have you ever heard the Tablet of Ahmad? (p. 170, center) In what language(s)?

⇨ Read the Tablet of Ahmad. Found in most Bahá'í prayer books and at **http://reference.bahai.org/en/t/c/BP/bp-173.html** . Discuss.

💬 What do you think of Abby's idea that these special Divine Messengers are very much alike? (pp. 172, 5th ¶ from bottom and p. 172, ¶ 6)

💬 ⓘ Do you have a Last Will and Testament? (p. 173, last ¶) It's good for everyone to write down how your possessions should be disposed of, and any wishes you have for your funeral service, burial and headstone, even if you're young; none of us knows when we'll move on to the next world. Bahá'ís are also urged to have a spiritual testimony; discuss and look at examples.

©2021 Lisa Bradley Godward/ Wize Media
Reproduction for personal/fair use only

⇨ If you don't have a will (and testament), write one, however informal. (It needs to go through a few more legal steps to hold up in court, etc., but the author feels that something is better than nothing, and we can make final plans even when young.) Store it safely and tell someone you trust where it is.

💬 The author chose the word "ma'rifat" instead of "grok" from Robert Heinlein's *Stranger in a Strange Land.* (pp. 174, ¶ 3-6) Both words get at this idea of thoroughly understanding something until it is a part of you. What other words in other languages convey the same concept? ⌨

💬 ⇨ Have you ever seen someone walking in an ordinary situation with extraordinary grace? (p. 174, 3rd ¶ from bottom) The author has met several Native Americans and ballet dancers who moved with dignity and grace. Mother has been trying to train Abby and Jenn to move gracefully; now Abby sees a number of examples in Erden. Act out or demonstrate graceful walking, sitting, etc.

💬 From the Erdean actress's description of 'Abdu'l-Bahá, do you wish you could have met him when he was alive? (pp. 174-177) If you could meet him now, how would you use that opportunity, i.e., ask certain questions, give him something, show him something? Is there another now-deceased historical figure you wish you could spend time with?

💬 Share your favorite stories of spiritual, inspiring peoples' lives, from any faith or tradition. Tell why a story is meaningful to you.

💬 Abby is uplifted and ennobled by hearing about 'Abdu'l-Bahá . Share your thoughts after p. 177.

💬 ⓘ Look at photographs and sketches of 'Abdu'l-Bahá. [Follow link in Book Endnote 109 to see Gibran's sketch of him; also enter his name in Google, then click on Images.] Discuss.

Chapter 24: Animals

💬 Which types of plants and flowers attract what kind of flutteries? (p. 179, second-to-last ¶) Earthers already plant gardens to attract specific creatures. Name some more.

⇨ ⓘ Watch some videos of hummingbirds. (p. 179, last ¶) Try to watch ones that capture the whirring sound of their wings. Listen to Seals and Crofts' spiritually-inspired song, "Hummingbird." Are you are attracted by hummingbirds or other animals enough to draw, photograph, write, or research them?

💬 Abby feels spiritually "reborn," and remembers hearing about it in church. **Reference Guide Endnote 3.** (p. 179, ¶1) Discuss: can any of you identify with this? What do different faiths say about this? What causes people to feel this way?

💬 What do you think of the WaerY camera? (p. 179, middle half)

⇨ Draw the scenes the WaerY might have captured. Even stick figures can convey a visual idea. (p. 180) ⌨ 📷

⇨ Act out the horse and handlers' warmup exercises (pp. 179-180); one person be the horse, the other be the handler, then switch.

💬 Do you think the birds are well-trained real birds, or are they some kind of technology? (p. 181, second-to-last ¶ and others)

💬 Share your thoughts about the animal show. (pp. 180-185) Could you imagine all the motions? Did you like it or not? Why or why not? ⌨

💬 What do you think about the Honor accorded to the performers afterwards? (p. 185, ¶2-4)

⇨ Act out the "Singing Honor" scene. 📷

💬 Name some promising lives ruined by fame. (p. 185, second-to-last ¶)

💬 Why *are* Americans so into autographs and fan clubs? Why *do* we lose it when we have the chance to meet a real celebrity? (p. 186, ¶2) Daniel Radcliffe even said on Larry King, 7/15/11, the day the last *Harry Potter* film came out, that Americans do this more than Brits.

💬 Why might Dali have withheld the information about the one trainer? (pp. 186, middle of page, and 188, last few ¶)

💬 Discuss the explanation Farrah gives about hanging out with horses. (p. 186, second-to-last ¶)

💬 Speculate how the plate and stovetop work. (p. 187, fourth-from-bottom ¶) ⌨

💬 Do you think horses can smile? (p. 187, third-from-last ¶) What about other animals' facial expressions?

©2021 Lisa Bradley Godward/ Wize Media
Reproduction for personal/fair use only

⇨ Draw one of your own Steeds of Faith, or even order a kit from Trail of Painted Ponies **www.TrailofPaintedPonies.com** or perhaps the Breyer "Paint Your Own Horse" kit, and make a Steed of Faith, whether like the one in the book or different. (p. 188, last few ¶ onto p. 189, top) 🖮 🎥

Chapter 25: School

💬 Which of the happiness quotes is your favorite? (pp. 153-154, 155, 162, 168, 186, 187, 191) Why?

💬 Describe the Peace Corps to any in your Group who don't know what it is. (p. 191, second-to-last ¶) **www.PeaceCorps.gov** . Would you like to do that or not? How is Citizenship Service Year different from Peace Corps?

💬 How do Americans often meet their spouses now? Do you think getting to know possible future spouses on Citizenship Service Year is better or worse than the usual ways? (p. 192, ¶3-5)

⇨ Act out Abby's fantasy on page 192. Use whatever props you wish, or pretend it all.

💬 What do you think of *Saġo Supera Lernejo*'s welcome sign? (p. 193, black box) Have you seen evidence of the truth of this in your life or the life of someone you know? This Activity & Discussion Guide has been aimed at helping uncover some of your gems. Has it helped you find some? 🖮 🎥

💬 Discuss the "guidance" regarding adornments on p. 194, ¶2. How can a person wear things or enjoy the earth's benefits without letting any of it get in the way of their relationship with God? Is this why the poor are mentioned favorably in several of the world's religions?

ⓘ 💬 Search for references to the poor in various religions and philosophies. Each one of you could take a different religion and investigate, possibly in printed religious concordances that list scriptures by topic such as *Strong's Concordance* for the Bible and Heggie's *Index of Quotations From the Bahá'í Sacred Writings.* Compare quotes, then discuss.

💬 What benefits would children gain who studied animals from their earliest days? (p. 195, ¶10)

💬 Abby wonders about ways to skip school and is told that students wouldn't want to. (pp. 195, last two ¶, and p. 196, first three ¶) If your school was like *Saĝo Supera Lernejo*, would you love school too? Why or why not? Discuss your ideal vision of a school. 🖼️

💬 Mr. Wells: is that his calling name or not? (p. 196, ¶ 9)

💬 The idea for Testing Lab (p. 196, ¶4 and third from bottom; pp. 199, third ¶ from bottom, through p. 200, last ¶) came from the author's father, who described an engineering course in the 1940's nicknamed "The Busting Lab." She also drew from Adib Taherzadeh's recorded talks, *Drawing Nigh Unto Bahá'u'lláh*, in which he says that the material world reflects the spiritual world; everything in that world has a physical counterpart or representation on earth. "The first proof is that the outward is the expression of the inward: The earthly realm is the mirror of the heavenly Kingdom, and the material world is in accordance with the spiritual world."– 'Abdu'l-Baha, *Some Answered Questions*, p. 283. What other materials can you envision the students testing in Testing Lab? What might be the results, and what spiritual properties might have been explored as analogies? 🖼️

ⓘ 💬 Research and discuss the persecution of various religions' founders and the early believers. (p. 196, last three ¶, and top half of p. 197) If you like, read and discuss the *Kitab-i-Iqan*, (Book of Certitude), which discusses this repeating dynamic.

➡️ ⓘ Do a bit of yoga. (p. 198 and top half of p. 199) If one of your Group knows some yoga moves, have them show you some, or arrange for an instructor. Never push yourself past your limits. Even gentle stretches can be helpful. Look up some of the different kinds of yoga and understand the differences. Explore and enjoy yoga's Hindu tie-in.

➡️ Draw or otherwise dramatize Petra's analogy of spiritual ink on a spiritual surface increasing spiritual strength. (p. 200, top half) 🎨

💬 What unusual uses for paper can you think of? (p. 200, sixth-from-the-last ¶)

➡️ Take Mr Wells' challenge; can you build a structure that will hold you 20 cm off the floor for 10 seconds? Use Dali's suggestion and use many small pyramids or bricks. (p. 200, second-to-last ¶) If you know any engineers, ask them for help in the calculations so you waste less time and/or paper.

💬 Is Ms. Reed, the *Insrtu Gentilajo*, using a calling name or not? (p. 201, middle of page)

💬 Name some academic pursuits you think begin and end in words. (p. 201, third-from-last ¶)

💬 What would your sparks be made of? (pp. 196, second-to-last ¶; 197, middle of page; and 202, ¶ 3)

💬 Discuss the "little voice" of divine guidance. (p. 202, ¶5) Do we all have it? If you like, share some instances you felt it in action, whether or not you listened and benefitted from it.

💬 Without griping, have you been deeply hurt by a thoughtless comment, or felt unheard when sharing something deep? (p. 202, last three ¶, and onto p. 203, first ¶) How can you avoid doing the same thing to someone else? Is there anything you can do once you were hurt to try to get satisfaction?

💬 Abby makes a new saying ("You can lead a horse to wonders, but you cannot make it think.") from an old one. What is the old saying she's changed? (p. 203, third ¶ from bottom)

⇨ Draw or otherwise dramatize Ms. Reed's horses analogy. (p. 204, ¶3) 🎭

⇨ What issues do you wish you had handled better, or need help to handle well? (pp. 203-204) Is there a conversation you know you need to have with someone, but have been putting off because you don't know how, or fear it will go badly? Find someone(s) who can help you get your heart and head in a good place to have that talk. Often, we have underlying anxiety, fear or distress that blocks us coming from a position of patience, love, etc. Can your "ungripe session" partner help you identify your worries first, deal with them, then decide on wording and even possible solutions to discuss with the person in question? Feel free to use Lisa Bradley Godward's *Applied Bahá'í Consultation* outline, summarized in this Guide's Endnote #1, and also at **www.amazon.com/dp/B077SM43T6** .

💬 📖 Discuss 'Abdu'l-Bahá's quote on p. 205, in the box. Is this helpful guidance? Why or why not? Could it change how you handle something in the future?

💬 Discuss the next boxed quote by Ruhiyyih Rabbani (*roo-HEE-yah rah-BONNIE*). (p. 206, ¶2)

Chapter 26: Lunch

❓ 💬 Notice the 9-pointed star illustration on p. 176, on the spine of the Revised Edition, and possibly the design on p. 207, ¶ 6. Author Lisa Bradley Godward has chosen this as the "Abby Wize Star." What other stars, religious symbols and uplifting stained glass works might there be in the windows? (p. 207, ¶ 6) ✉

💬 ⇨ Would you like to visit, or have you been to, a Tranquility Zone or something like it? (pp. 207-208) Discuss, share photos, Google, draw or create an actual one.

⇨ Eat, or discuss eating, as a vegan (*VEE*-gen; no animal products) for a day or more. (p. 208, fifth ¶ from bottom; middle of p. 209, and others).

💬 ⇨ "The Princess And The Pea" refers to a well-known fable. (p. 209, third ¶ from bottom) Read it, then discuss as it relates to Vivian Wize's attitude towards her daughter.

💬 Do you or anyone you know have any of the conditions listed on pp. 210, ¶ 3? What is said to be the cause? What is the cure, if any? What do these folks have to do to manage their condition? Look at Book Endnotes 141-145. Research and discuss any aspects that interest you.

⇨ Write the quote on p. 211, ¶5, in calligraphy or nice handwriting. Decorate attractively. First, look at and discuss attractive examples of calligraphy and decorative artwork around the words. [The author's favorite living calligrapher is the Turk, Muhammed Bastag. YouTube videos available. A famous Bahá'í calligrapher to research is Mishkin-Qalam.] Each person can do an individual project, or see if you want to collaborate, with two or more of you working together on one project. If someone has nice handwriting, let them do that part; if someone draws well, they can do that part; if someone has an eye for the layout/design, let them suggest the layout. Or learn and enjoy as you go!

💬 Discuss the quote shining on the cafeteria's waterfall. (p. 211, seventh ¶ from the bottom)

💬 Add your thoughts to the discussion on premarital sex. (pp. 212-214)

💬 Would there be actual nurses in Erdean schools? (p. 215) Would they wear white? (p. 215, ¶ 6)

💬 Why might Petra fumble her words, when normally she's so poised? (p. 215, ¶8)

💬 What are your feelings at arriving back with Jenn? (p. 216)

Chapter 27: Return

💬 Is this (p. 217, second ¶ from bottom) what Reverend Davison meant when he talked about rapture (pp. 23-24) or is that something else?

⇨ Abby might have been able to easily calculate how many weeks it had been (p. 218, ¶6) if she'd been taught how to multiply on her fingers, such as shown in **https://www.parent24.com/Learn/Back-to-School/maths-finger-calculations-the-indian-way-20170227**

💬 How do you feel when reading what Abby misses about Erden? (p. 219, ¶5 and others)

💬 ⓘ What are some happy thoughts that might make you fly, like in *Hook*? (p. 219, ¶5) If you haven't seen that movie yet, watch it, possibly as a group.

⇨ Sing the first prayer at the bottom of p. 219. Find numerous versions on YouTube; search "Remover of Difficulties" and enjoy! One of author Lisa Bradley Godward's favorites is **http://www.youtube.com/watch?v=gbltR8CNH18&NR=1** .

⇨ Sing the second prayer at the bottom of p. 219. One version author Lisa Bradley Godward likes is at **http://www.youtube.com/watch?v=TQZIUJ18xaY&feature=related** . Note that many faiths have posted healing prayers on YouTube.

💬 ⓘ What do you know about the stories of people who've died and come back? (p. 220, ¶8) There are websites to read more stories, if you wish, such as **http://www.near-death.com** . Author Lisa Bradley Godward feels that these accounts often match up quite accurately with Bahá'í descriptions of the next worlds.

⇨ Sing or listen to Toko Zani, (p. 221) perhaps at **http://www.youtube.com/watch?v=cF_dIME8b_Q** .

💬 Do you notice any similarities between the scenes on pages 222 and 119? Discuss.

💬 In way(s) do you think *kam, kam, ruz bih ruz* would be useful in your life? (p. 224, second ¶ from bottom)

Chapter 28: Phonecall

💬 ⓘ Jenn reports seeing Abby far ahead in dreams, laughing. (p. 225, ¶3) Discuss and/or research dreams and their position in our practical and spiritual life.

💬 Discuss Melissa's statement that the essence of all the religions is truly the same. (p. 226, ¶3-5)

➪ Write a list of virtues, then write their contra-virtues (the author's word) next to each item, i.e., Greed = Appetite. Stubbornness = Persistence. Selfishness = Self-Preservation. (p. 228, ¶5) Several resources available free, including a list of virtues, at **https://www.virtuesproject.com/virtueslist.html** .

💬 ➪ Discuss and/or roleplay situations in which one person backbites or gossips maliciously about another, and you redirect or address the gossip. (pp. 227-228)

➪ Draw the two visions of Heaven on Earth mentioned on p. 229, ¶5. 📷

💬 Discuss Abby's relationship with her mother. (p. 229, middle of the page, and many others) What do you think might be Abby's mental process in this scene, and what do you think about it?

💬 Name more ways in which Abby is similar to Harry. (p. 231, bottom half) How are you similar to either Abby or Harry?

💬 What do you think could have caused Mother to be the way she is? (p. 233, ¶ 1)

💬 Do you think Abby's little voice is the same as her gut feelings? (p. 233, second-to-last ¶) Discuss.

💬 Abby reads "Let your vision be world-embracing, rather than confined to your own self." She hears the words "World-embracing" and "vision" faintly in Dali's voice. (p. 234, third ¶ from the bottom) Could this be what Dali was trying to say on p. 80, ¶2? If not, what was she trying to say?

💬 Discuss Abby's praying and willpower on p. 235, top half of the page. Is this progress in her spiritual quest, or not? What does spiritual capacity look like? What are some steps in that direction? What might your next step look like?

💬 Discuss the common practice of hazing at schools. (p. 236, last four ¶) What can be done about it?

Chapter 29: Reentry

⇨ ⓘ Develop the details of the notation system Abby might have used, and/or one that's useful to you. (p. 237, first ¶) Explore shorthand notation and learn a word or two in it. Gregg Shorthand is the most common system. ⌨ 📷

⇨ Look at the shortest of the three obligatory prayers. **Endnote 4 of this Guide.** (p. 237, second ¶ from bottom) Say it if you wish. What other faiths have similar prescribed prayers?

⇨ Learn about the persecution of Bahá'ís and adherents of other religions, (p. 238, ¶2) perhaps using such resources as **http://en.wikipedia.org/wiki/Persecution_of_Bah%C3%A1%27%C3%ADs** .

💬 What are Bahá'í Covenant Breakers? (pp. 238-239) Is there an equivalent in other religions? How are Covenant Breakers similar to Death Eaters in *Harry Potter?* How are they dissimilar?

💬 What is your Gunsmoke (at school, work, home or other?) (p. 240, ¶3) This could mean a spiritual test, a challenge, or anything else you don't know how to handle.

💬 ⇨ What might Erdean books contain? Do they still have paper books then? Or are books all electronic? (p. 240, ¶4) Make or describe some possibilities. ⌨ 📷

⇨ Abby finds herself between two worlds (p. 240, second-to-last ¶): when she was in Erden, Earth leaked through occasionally. (pp. 83, ¶8; 86, ¶ 7; 101, ¶8; 167, ¶10; and others) Now that she's back in Earth, Erden bleeds through occasionally. Write more fan-fic scenes in which one or the other world bleeds through. ⌨

💬 How has Abby's view of happiness evolved over the course of her adventures? (p. 243, ¶6)

⇨ Collect your own happiness quotes or thoughts in addition to those in the novel. What simple things might you do to increase your happiness, such as laugh with friends, see a beautiful sky, smell something wonderful? Many people find that by finding things to be grateful for, and even keeping a Gratitude Journal, their happiness increases. Do you think these activities would bring you more happiness than buying or owning things? Why or why not?

⇨ Write a more detailed scene based on p. 243, second ¶ from the bottom, of the insights Abby might have been getting lost in.

💬 What "candles" could Abby use in her battle against the darkness? (p. 245, ¶ 2)

⇨ Draw the Draggin' Dragon, and any other scenes you wish. (p. 246) Center yourself first, to try to channel guidance and the delight of creating.

Chapter 30: Sunday

💬 Discuss Jenn's statement that "Jesus is the only way" and Abby's view that all of the founders of the world's major religions were the only way, each for their time and place. (p. 247, ¶1 & 2)

💬 What should be done to build greater religious tolerance in the world? (p. 247, ¶3) What can you do?

💬 ⇨ Abby instinctively knows that Mother is racially prejudiced. (p. 248, ¶2-4) Why does Abby disagree, even though normally, parents' attitudes are ingrained into the children? What could Abby have said to address Mother's prejudice? Rewrite the scene to include Abby addressing Mother's racism in a way that Mother might have been able to take in.

💬 Abby has been in a low-key war with Mother most of her life. But the Bahá'í and other faiths say war is bad. Might Abby be able to use Melissa's idea of contra-virtues and decide that war against some wrong things is the right approach? (p. 248, ¶ 4)

💬 Why would a long dress and elbow-length gloves made in Erden have kept Abby cooler than capris and polo shirt in Tennessee? (p. 248, second ¶ from bottom)

⇨ Act out the scene of LaKeesha asking Abby polite questions about her knowledge of the Bahá'í Faith, and Abby trying to avoid mentioning anything that would reveal her trip to Erden. (p. 249, bottom half)

⇨ On YouTube, find examples and sing "Look At Me," "Magic Penny," "Educate These Children" and "Shine Your Light on Me," pp. 250-251. "Look At Me": **http://www.youtube.com/watch?v=iPNEm295WK4** . "Shine Your Light": **http://www.youtube.com/watch?v=AE25CdEjuH4** For a high-tech, hip-hop version of "Educate These Children," visit **http://www.youtube.com/watch?v=dVqlrjuaFCU** .

⇨ What would the animated Yuter presentations contain? (p. 252, ¶ 1) Use whatever mode (write, act out, draw, etc.) would best convey your concept. 📻 📹

⇨ Draw the children's drawings from the top half of page 252. Or find or invent your own images for how to stay connected to God, and draw them. [Such as, pointing a spiritual satellite dish towards God to receive Sia signals.] 📹

⇨ ⓘ Read the ingredients on an average container of fruit punch and sugar cookies. (p. 252, ¶4) Identify the chemicals, colorings, additives, etc. Look up the known bad effects of the ingredients you find. What would more acceptable alternatives be? Would kids like them? Why or why not? Provide healthy snacks you think the kids will eat at gatherings that include children. Discuss this with the parents and the children ahead of time and during the gathering.

💬 Brainstorm possible ideas that the Surely believers could have contributed toward the question, "What techniques do you use to stay as connected to the Divine as possible?" (p. 252, ¶ 5)

💬 ⇨ Discuss Abby's illumined outlook on her not-yet-harmonious Surely Bahá'í community. (pp. 253-254) Is this an approach you think you can use when things don't go ideally? Why or why not? How would changing your thoughts change your attitude? Decide on some possible approaches you can take with people you don't get along with (yet). Optional: make a card, page or poster with these decisions.

💬 What can you do to nudge your spiritual community's activities closer to the much-awaited time of Heaven on Earth? (p. 254)

💬 Besides Dali and the others in Erden counting on Abby and her struggling friends, what other good reasons can you think of for Abby (and us) to contribute our best efforts to the building of that glorious Golden Age? (p. 254)

-END OF ACTIVITY & DISCUSSION GUIDE-

©2021 Lisa Bradley Godward/ Wize Media
Reproduction for personal/fair use only

After you finish the Activity & Discussion Guide

💬 ⇨ Go back and complete the activities with the 📖 icon.

💬 Speculate: In Erden, are there gas stations? Grocery stores? Post offices? Mail? What do you think cars will look like/be made of? ⌨️ 🎥

⇨ Draw Abby 🎥

💬 ⓘ Find your favorite sentence ⌨️

💬 Describe your favorite scene ⌨️

⇨ Write another fanfiction scene that could be in the book but is not. ⌨️

💬 ⇨ List your favorite Erdean inventions/gadgets. Invent a few more, keeping in mind Dali's description of appropriate use of technology. (pp. 110; and 164, around bottom third of page)

💬 Name a pet peeve or problem in the world now and play one of Abby's games: "How would this be handled in Erden?" (p. 240, ¶ 5)

💬 Decide on a topic you'd like to discuss with author Lisa Bradley Godward and see about having her attend one of your sessions to discuss it. 📧

©2021 Lisa Bradley Godward/ Wize Media
Reproduction for personal/fair use only

How to Spread the Word About *Abby Wize*

Most importantly, tell others about this (unfortunately) rare point of view: a harmonious, realistic portrayal of humanity at peace in the future.
- Post a positive review on *Abby*'s Amazon page. If you've bought more than $50 from Amazon in the last year, they'll let you post a review, even if you didn't get your book from Amazon. These reviews are crucial to future buyers/readers. (And feel free to email author Lisa Bradley Godward at **grow@wize.media** with things you didn't like much.)
- FRIEND and LIKE the two Abby Wize Facebook pages, so you can mention, tag, repost, share, or any other connections and descriptions you can make respectfully on social media. Facebook is particularly productive for discussing *Abby*.
    - Facebook personal page: Abby Wize.
    - Fan/business page: Abby Wize Media.
- FOLLOW Abby Wize on Twitter, and retweet, or generate your own tweets and tag Abby.
- Download and print bookmarks to hand out. Go to **www.wize.media/more** and scroll to "Download."
- Suggest *Abby Wize – AWAY* to friends, family, colleagues, book clubs, women's groups, teen groups, churches, mosques, synagogues, and other religious groups; university and high school classes; groups interested in peace, education, reduction of crime, animals and animal-whispering, and any others that have something in common with *Abby*'s themes.
- Gather names of people with whom you talk about it, and follow up after what seems like an appropriate interval.
- Look for interested people and be prepared to talk with them.
- Practice describing the book briefly and concisely. The author's description, which she memorized and says with a smile: "It's a novel about a horse-loving teen's spiritual visit to a future age of World Peace." Give them a chance to register what you've said, and listen to their comments and questions. If they say, as so many have, "Oh, wow!" and remain interested, your next sentence could be, "It's the first

in a series that's going to include a lot of different faiths, races, and nations in a peaceful way." If they ask which faiths, you could mention that the first book includes Episcopalian, Native American, Bahá'í, and mentions all the world's major religions in a positive way. If they ask what Bahá'í is, feel free to use Ms. Godward's carefully crafted short description: "It's a wonderful world-wide religion working for world peace." Just remember all the W's and start with "wonderful."

- o To make *Abby* more widely available and remove one financial barrier, buy and place a copy(s) in your public or religious library(s), or provide them with the ISBN number so they can. Libraries prefer hardbound copies because they wear better. The ISBN for the *Abby Wize – AWAY* hardcover version is 978-1733327626 . **Note**: library books must be checked out at least once a year in order not to be culled and sold at the Friends of Library sales. Someone(s) need to check on your book to either make sure it has been checked out, or to check it out yourself(s). **Also note** that almost all libraries are part of a special nationwide loaning system called the Interlibrary Loan system, or ILL. This enables someone wanting *Abby Wize* to borrow it from a library far away, thereby vastly increasing the reach of each book placed in public libraries.
- o Suggest *Abby Wize* to any bloggers, vloggers, newspaper book review columnists, radio shows, podcasts or any other media. Author Lisa Bradley Godward is happy to give interviews with a variety of slants: peace, horses, youth, girls, education, health, writing, and more. Give serious inquirers the email **grow@wize.media** .

Use these as springboards to your own ideas, and post them on Abby's Facebook pages. ⌨

Endnotes to this Guide
(Not the same as the novel's Endnotes):

Endnote 1. Here's a checklist of steps to action-oriented group consultation that Author Lisa Bradley Godward developed (see her *Wise Utterance* Compilation for more on speech and utterance, or the excerpted *Applied Bahá'í Consultation* for a little more on her version of Bahá'í Consultation):

> Prep: Prepare spiritually. Pray, think about being open to the best answer, not to "getting your way." Look forward to seeking the truth in the consultation and to hearing/realizing Divine guidance when meeting with the others.

1. Frame the problem/situation as accurately as possible. See if you can form it into a question, and if it's a project, start with "how," i.e., "How can we do this?"
2. Fact-find so that you have the necessary figures, feelings and preferences, resources, etc. available. (Consultation goes faster and smoother if someone has already done steps 2 and 3 before the meeting.) Identify the root purpose, operating principles, and goals. Refer to these when things get convoluted.
3. Brainstorm possible answers prayerfully, turning to God for answers. If ideas have any possible element of usefulness, seize that bit. Pray during this part; often, even words you *thought* someone else was going to say can be useable!
4. Decide on a course of action. When voting, a unanimous vote is preferable; if not, then majority rules. Everyone supports the majority vote; there are no dissenting votes. If it doesn't work out after trying it in good faith, the later assessment will reveal the need for adjustments. [Ms. Godward's definition of a plan is: Everyone involved knows who's going to do what, when, how, where (and why, if applicable).]
5. Divide the tasks, aiming for the division most likely to result in success. Volunteering is good.
6. Observe how the plan is unfolding as you pursue it; adjust as needed at the time, consulting people who have skills and insight regarding the issue at hand.

©2021 Lisa Bradley Godward/ Wize Media
Reproduction for personal/fair use only

7. If it's an ongoing project, set aside time to meet and review events. Identify what's working, and why; what's not working, and why. Revise the plans as needed to carry out the principles, goals and purposes and/or revise the goals.

Repeat any/all steps as needed, striving to keep love, unity, peacefulness, and other collaborative qualities foremost.

Endnote 2. In a letter written on his behalf, Shoghi Effendi said: "We must take the teachings as a great, balanced whole, not seek out and oppose to each other two strong statements that have different meanings; somewhere in between, there are links uniting the two." Quoted in **http://www.bahai.org/library/authoritative-texts/the-universal-house-of-justice/messages/#d=19950427_001&f=fl**

Endnote 3. From the Bible: John 3:3 Jesus answered and said unto him, Verily, verily, I say unto thee, Except a man be born again, he cannot see the kingdom of God.
3:4 Nicodemus saith unto him, How can a man be born when he is old? can he enter the second time into his mother's womb, and be born? 3:5 Jesus answered, Verily, verily, I say unto thee, Except a man be born of water and of the Spirit, he cannot enter into the kingdom of God.
3:6 That which is born of the flesh is flesh; and that which is born of the Spirit is spirit.
3:7 Marvel not that I said unto thee, Ye must be born again.
3:8 The wind bloweth where it listeth, and thou hearest the sound thereof, but canst not tell whence it cometh, and whither it goeth: so is every one that is born of the Spirit.
3:9 Nicodemus answered and said unto him, How can these things be? 3:10 Jesus answered and said unto him, Art thou a master of Israel, and knowest not these things? 3:11 Verily, verily, I say unto thee, We speak that we do know, and testify that we have seen; and ye receive not our witness.
3:12 If I have told you earthly things, and ye believe not, how shall ye believe, if I tell you of heavenly things? 3:13 And no man hath ascended up to heaven, but he that came down from heaven, even the Son of man which is in heaven.

3:14 And as Moses lifted up the serpent in the wilderness, even so must the Son of man be lifted up: 3:15 That whosoever believeth in him should not perish, but have eternal life.

Endnote 4. Short obligatory prayer, to be recited once in twenty-four hours, at noon:
> I bear witness, O my God, that Thou hast created me to know Thee and to worship Thee. I testify, at this moment, to my powerlessness and to Thy might, to my poverty and to Thy wealth.
> There is none other God but Thee, the Help in Peril, the Self-Subsisting.
> -Baha'u'llah, *Prayers and Meditations by Baha'u'llah,* p. 313.

Discussion Suggestions
By Author Lisa Bradley Godward

I suggest limiting comments to 2 or 3 minutes. Adults especially can get a bit carried away with sharing.

I recommend a younger age limit of 12 or so, both for the book and for this Discussion Group. Younger children may get bored and then disruptive. But this wonderful book does lend itself well to a mixed-age, mixed-faith Discussion Group.

One strength of this Guide is that participants can, over time, note which topics and/or activities they like best or are best at. This could be a good clue about the innate strengths and abilities that can form a foundation for future careers and hobbies.

Although this is called a Discussion Guide, you could write or draw your answers. There is no single correct answer to any of the questions. The main goal is to enjoy your time together.

If a question or activity doesn't suit your Group's "groupanality," skip it. Or substitute your own invention. ⌨ If you don't finish a chapter or a question and want to, simply pick it up next time.

The wishes of the majority should almost always dictate the direction of the Group, except if unsafe or if, for example, one very vocal person keeps steering the Group his or her way.

If some members find the pace a little slow but the majority enjoys the pace, encourage activities for the waiting ones. Knit or do other fiber arts (try the counted cross-stitch in the back of the novel); doodle (research Zentangles and try those); draw (especially something from the book); catch up on homework/paperwork and hop in later; post an update to the **Abby Wize** OR **Abby Wize Media** Facebook pages (photographs of your activities are great; just get permission of everyone appearing in the photo). I hope each Group member will help make the Group enjoyable.

If people want to read ahead in the book, please respect anyone who doesn't want "Plot Spoilers" – revealing what happens in the book.

<u>Group Leaders</u>: I suggest you have a Discussion Leader, a Curriculum Monitor, and a Communicator. People can have more

than one job, if that works better. Use whatever structure suits your Group. The designated positions could be elected or volunteer; could stay the same for a time or change every week.

Discussion Leader: prevents Group apathy due to domination by a minority. Keeps the discussion moving along, allowing for input as long as there is interest in a topic by the majority. Runs a timer if necessary to limit comments to 2 or 3 minutes per person. Scouts out and arranges meeting places, remembering that Group meetings might include activities that need certain types of venues (facilities) such as ones that allow easy cleanup after art projects, or are big enough to move around for the acting activities. Realizes that silence often indicates thinking, which is good!

Curriculum Monitor: scans the upcoming questions and activities in advance of the next Group meeting. Coordinates with Leader. Notifies Group members or the Communicator about the section of the book that will likely be covered at the next meeting and communicates this to the Group Members, so as many people as possible will have read it (if reading for the first time). See what supplies will be needed, then notify Group members or the Communicator about these supplies.

Communicator: emails and/or phones people with meeting dates, places, times, changes, and supply notices. Gathers input ("votes") on questions to determine the majority preference. You can start your own Abby Wize Facebook page – just give it a name different from the official ones, such as "Anytown Abby Wize Book Club" – and conduct Polls there for an easy way to find out what the Group wants to do (assuming everyone in your Group joins that page).

Ms. Godward feels strongly that no one should be coerced into sharing if they don't want to. Invited or encouraged, yes, but we should be able to choose whether and when we participate. Hopefully everyone comes because they feel valued and respected, and they'll share when they're ready. In keeping with this idea, things that people share about themselves should not be repeated outside the Group. Ideas, devoid of personal details, might be suitable for repeating. 🐾 ⇨ Members might need help in learning about and practicing these confidentiality skills.

An internet connection will help you look up links and do searches during meetings, if that's how you decide to handle the internet research. Many libraries, McDonalds, and Starbucks have free wifi to use with an internet-capable device. However, you may want to rotate your meeting places according to the upcoming activities/projects. This could work well, because when curious people ask what you're doing, you can tell them about this fabulous book: "It's about a 13-year-old horse-loving girl who is suddenly thrown into the far future, when World Peace has finally arrived!" Then wait for their inevitable reply: "Wow! Cool!" or "That's not going to happen anytime soon!" And you reply, "Yeah, the author put it at 700 years in the future, but she shows why we need to start now!"

All of you are welcome to consider yourselves Abby Wize Promoters. See the previous section on "How to Promote Abby Wize" for a few ideas on spreading the word. Feel free to come up with your own. ⌨ Hurray for a beautiful future!

It's possible that one person could form a Group and do all the activities. It's also possible to have an online or internet group. Ms. Godward will do what she can to assist the formation of internet groups, or go ahead and post an invitation(s) to the official Abby Wize Facebook and Twitter pages.

Whether I've marked it to share on Facebook or not, please post insightful, fun and/or uplifting thoughts and pictures from your Group on "Abby Wize" and/or "Abby Wize Media" Facebook pages … and/or email them to through **www.wize.media**

Please leave positive reviews on the Amazon pages for *Abby Wize - AWAY* and for this *Activity and Discussion Guide*. Note the Z in Wize.
Abby Wize – AWAY, Amazon: **www.amazon.com/dp/1733327606**
Amazon listing for this Guide: **www.amazon.com/dp/1733327633**

©2021 Lisa Bradley Godward/ Wize Media
Reproduction for personal/fair use only

Notes

Notes